Foreword

by Roger McGough

Gyles Brandreth (Searchingly): 'REACH is a most worthy cause, is it not?'
Me (Suspiciously): 'Yes?'
G.B. (Conspiratorially): 'And we are patrons, are we not?'
Me (Softening): 'Yes?'
G.B. (Enlighteningly): 'Then let us produce a book of poems to raise money.'
Me (Enthusiastically): 'Yes!'

And so we did, and here it is. Some old and golden favourites as well as many you will be reading for the first time. Our thanks to all the contributors, be they poets, friends, or simply hugely-famous people, who took the time and the trouble to help.

Some folk sent in poems they had written themselves. Some sent us poems written by others. We have done our best to ensure that we have permission to reproduce all the poems, but if we have overlooked anybody do please let us know so we can put matters right.

By way of introduction and explanation, that's it. Now…

To set the poetry in motion, ten little poems that speak volumes…

YOUNG POETS

by Nicanor Parra
(Translated from the Spanish by Miller Williams)

Write as you will
In whatever style you like
Too much blood has run under the bridge
To go on believing
That only one road is right.

In poetry everything is permitted.

With only this condition, of course,
You have to improve the blank page.

WRITE ON!

by Martin Hall

I've been writing this poem
for two hours solid,
and I've only done three lines.

Oh, four.

THE FASTEST TRAIN IN THE WORLD

by Keith Bosley

Tokyo to Kyoto
tokyotokyoto
kyotokyotokyotokyo
tokyotokyoto

PENNIES FROM HEAVEN

by Spike Milligan

I put 10p in my Piggy Bank
To save for a rainy day.
It rained the *very next morning!*
Three Cheers, Hip Hip Hooray!

SILENCE:
by Les Coleman

place where libraries are built.

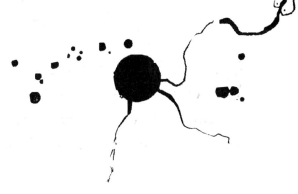

UNTITLED
by Eugen Gomringer

silencio silencio silencio
silencio silencio silencio
silencio   silencio
silencio silencio silencio
silencio silencio silencio

9

DON'T STEAL

by Ambrose Bierce

Don't steal; thou'lt never thus compete
Successfully in business. Cheat.

O
GL'RIA

by Ladislav Novák

THE HEN

by MacAnon

The hen it is a noble beast
But a cow is more forlorner
Standing lonely in a field
Wi' one leg at each corner.

FAMOUS LAST

by Billy Bee

Don't worry
Lightening
never strikes twice
In the same

Contributed poems

UNCLE EDITH

from (and by) Allan Ahlberg

This poem, I regret to say,
Is quite untrue.
Uncle was really Auntie, of course,
And, Edith, actually, Hugh.

SELECTION

from (and by) Joan Aiken

Tabbies and blacks are aloof and superior
Tortoiseshells feminine, winsome and coy
White, unless washed, won't adorn your interior
Siamese yowls all affection destroy

Greys are deceitful, remote, disingenuous
Owners of Persians are slaves to the comb
Manx are ungraceful and Maltese too strenuous
Marmalade cats are the cats for the home.

And a limerick by my father which I found written in pencil at the back of The Constant Nymph, *which he gave my mother for Christmas in 1924:*

A LIMERICK

There was an old man called Fitzurse
When asked what his line was, said, "Verse
    Advanced echolalia
    Has made me a failure
I'll be making up rhymes in my hearse."

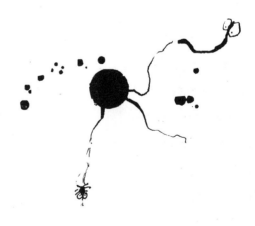

THE OTHER DAY

(Sister Wendy Beckett's choice)

The other day
Upon the stair
I met a man
Who wasn't there.
He isn't there
Again today
Oh! How I wish
He'd go away!

THREE RUTHLESS RHYMES

(Dickie Bird's choice)

I had written to Aunt Maud,
Who was on a trip abroad,
When I heard she'd died of cramp -
Just too late to save the stamp.

Llewelyn Peter James Maguire,
Touched a live electric wire;
Back on his heels it sent him rocking -
His language (like the wire) was shocking.

An accident happened to my brother Jim
When somebody threw a tomato at him -
Tomatoes are juicy, and don't hurt the skin,
But this one was specially packed in a tin.

THE DREADED DINOSAUR

from (and by) Val Biro

I am the dinosaur of dread,
The one you all supposed was dead!
Well, let me tell you here and now
That *this* Theropod's alive. And how!
So give me something fit to eat
Like half a ton of dripping meat!
Beware! I am a carnivore,
The terrible Tyrannosaur!

DEAREST DARLING DUCK

from (and by) Cilla Black

Dearest Darling Duck,
I send these sweets To Suck,
If one won't do,
Please Suck the two,
My Dearest Darling Duck!
Cilla Black

Lines from

THE SOLDIER

by Rupert Brooke
(Tony Blair's Choice)

If I should die, think only this of me:
That there's some corner of a foreign field
That is forever England. There shall be
In that rich earth a richer dust concealed;
A dust whom England bore, shaped, made aware,
Gave, once, her flowers to love, her ways to roam,
A body of England's, breathing English air,
Washed by the rivers, blest by suns of home.

JERRY HALL

(Quentin Blake's choice)

Jerry Hall
Is so small,
A rat could eat him
Hat and all.

UNTITLED

from (and by) David Blunkett

Too much I read of that which I have written
And if not written, wished that I had.
Too oft I hear the echo reflected
From the wall that I myself have built
And fail to recognise the words
Which bounce back in my face.

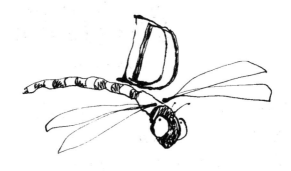

ANOTHER UNFORTUNATE CHOICE

by Wendy Cope
(Jo Brand's choice)

I think I am in love with A.E. Housman,
Which puts me in a worse-than-usual fix.
No woman ever stood a chance with Housman
And he's been dead since 1936.

UNTITLED

from (and by) Anthony Browne

At my birthday party
I had chocolate cake,
And cheesecake,
And fruitcake,
And ginger cake,
And fudge cake.
After that I had stummer cake.

A LITTLE WASP

from (and by) Alan Brownjohn

If a little wasp you see
Sipping at the jam at tea,
Think, before you treat him rough:
Do we feed our wasps enough?

My old school friend J.W. McCormick wrote a
favourite of mine (unpublished)
as follows:

A man named Schedlerup said to me,
"Dig that crazy apple-tree.
No! I don't mean dig it up.
Just perceive it."

LEARNING TO WALTZ...

from (and by) Amanda Butterworth, age 12
with just a little help from Dad,
(Nick Butterworth, age 47)

One two three,
One two three,
I can't dance,
Nor can he.

Oops ... bang, crash!
     Ouch! my toe...
       three
           four
               five...

One two three,
One two three,
I can't dance,
Nor can he.

GOING TOO FAR

by Wendy Cope
(Sir Hugh Casson's choice)

Cuddling the new telephone directory
After I found your name in it
Was going too far.
It's a safe bet you're not hugging a phone book,
Wherever you are.

SAUSAGES

(Billy Connolly's choice)

I'd rather be a sausage
Then a British Man of War,
Or a caterpillar with a broken arm.
Corduroy braces are all very well,
And give no immediate cause for alarm.
But the sausage is a mighty beast,
In fact, he is the mightiest there is
Content to lie in frying pans
Singing Sizzle Sizzle Sizzle Sizzle Sizz!

WHEN IN THE RING

from (and by) Henry Cooper

When In the Ring,
When In Doubt,
I always stuck my left out,

Henry Cooper

THE LOVER WRITES A ONE-WORD POEM

by Gavin Ewart
(Wendy Cope's choice)

You!

FOUR FEET

by Rudyard Kipling
(Ronnie Corbett's choice)

I have done mostly what most men do
And pushed it out of my mind
But I can't forget if I wanted to
Four feet trotting behind.

Day after day. The whole day through
Wherever my road inclined
Four feet said 'I am coming with you'
And trotted along behind.

Now I must go by some other road
A road I shall never find
Somewhere that does not carry the sound
Of four feet trotting behind.

BUS

from (and by) Iain Crichton Smith

There is no sorrow
worse than the sorrow
of seeing the last bus
draw away from the kerb.

THE PITY OF LOVE

by William Butler Yeats
(Frank Delaney's choice)

A pity beyond all telling
Is hid in the heart of love:
The folk who are buying and selling,
The clouds on their journey above,
The cold wet winds ever blowing,
And the shadowy hazel grove
Where mouse-grey waters are flowing,
Threaten the head that I love.

GLIMPSE

from (and by) Peter Dickinson

Bird or blown leaf? Look!
Quick! There! Gone
Before seen. Wren.
Was it?

FOR AN OLD MAN'S SUNDIAL

Also from (and by) Peter Dickinson

How slow the hours. How swift the years.
Time lags, drags, and dissapp

BABY

from (and by) Carol Ann Duffy

I like to rub noses with you.
I like to count toeses with you.
And what I supposes,
In fact I proposes
Wherever I goes it's with you.

THREE LIMERICKS

There was a young man from Bengal
Who went to a fancy dress ball.
    He thought he would risk it
    And go as a biscuit,
But a dog ate him up in the hall.

The bottle of perfume that Willie sent
Was highly displeasing to Millicent.
    Her thanks were so cold,
    They quarreled, I'm told,
Through that silly scent Willie sent Millicent.

A girl who weighed many oz.
Used language I dare not pronoz.
    For a fellow unkind
    Pulled her chair out behind
Just to see (so he said) if she'd boz.

RULES FOR COOKING TOAST

(Lindsay Fallow's choice)

Be accurate when cooking toast
Never try to guess
Cook it til it smokes and then
Twenty seconds less.

LOVE WITHOUT HOPE

by Robert Graves
(Anne Fine's choice)

Love without hope, as when the young bird-catcher
Swept off his tall hat to the Squire's own daughter,
So let the imprisoned larks escape and fly
Singing about her head, as she rode by.

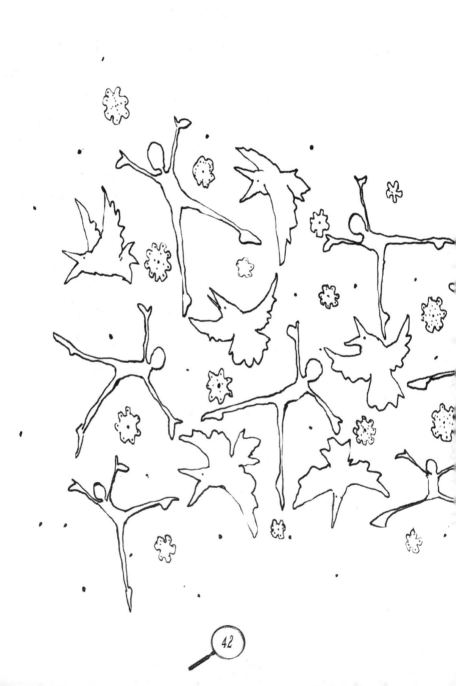

MOVEMENTS

from (and by) Nigel Forde

The snow is word perfect in a hundred different
                                        silences;
Steels itself for the soundless porcelain of an
                                        early moon.
And over locked lakes, barnyard, copse, come the
                                        unhindered birds,
Strange winter fruit, lending weight to bare branches.

TO MY MOTHER

by Robert Louis Stevenson
(Michael Foreman's choice)

You, too, my mother, read my rhymes
For the love of unforgotten times,
And you may chance to hear once more
The little feet along the floor.

LAST NIGHT

(Dawn French's choice)

Last night I slew my wife
Stretched her on the parquet flooring
I was loth to take her life
But I *had* to stop her snoring.

A FISHY THOUGHT

from (and by) Vivian French

A kipper
With a zipper
Would be neater
For the eater...

HE MIGHT HAVE LOOKED BETTER IN A BEARD

by Adrian Mitchell
(Martyn Goff's choice)

Philip Larkin
Was Chairman of the University of Hull
                    Committee on Parking
Thinking about and drinking about his
                    own demise
He was like Eric Morecambe without
                    benefit of Ernie Wise.

47

LITTLE LAMB

from (and by) Mike Harding

Little lamb who squashed thee?
Dost thou know who squashed thee?
Knocked thee down and squashed thee flat?
Sports car driven by a tourist pratt.
Baa Baa Broom Broom splatt!
Little lamb he squashed thee.

UNTITLED

from (and by) Rolf Harris

He'd paid his debt to society
His sentence was over at last
He collected his meagre belongings
And said goodbye to his past
The bars clanged shut behind him
As he stepped through the prison door
"I'm free," he shouted, "I'm free, I'm free!"
A little kid said, "I'm four!"

CHRISTMAS

from (and by) John Hegley

There came three wisemen from the East
and so it came to pass
the wisemen found the shepherds
a bit working class.

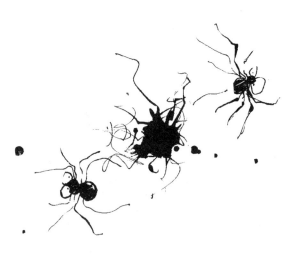

SHORT POEM

from (and by) Adrian Henri

I'm the shortest
in our year.
If you wrote a poem
about me
it'd only reach
to here ...

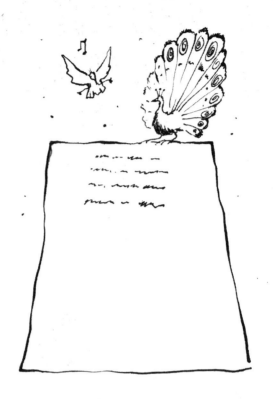

QUATRAIN

by Rumi
(Tobias Hill's choice)

Don't spend too much time with nightingales
and peacocks:
One is just a voice, the other only colour.

THE OPTIMIST AND THE PESSIMIST

by McLandburgh Wilson
(Glenn Hoddle's choice)

Twixt the optimist and pessimist
The difference is droll;
The optimist sees the doughnut,
The pessimist sees the hole.

MRS DARWIN

by Carol Ann Duffy
(Nick Hornby's choice)

7 April 1852
Went to the Zoo
I said to Him -
Something about that Chimpanzee over
there reminds me of you

WALKING AWAY

(on watching his child go to school for the first time)
by Cecil Day Lewis
(Nerys Hughes's choice)

I have had worse partings, but none that so
Gnaws at my mind still. Perhaps it is roughly
Saying what God alone could perfectly show -
How selfhood begins with a walking away,
And love is proved in the letting go.

UNTITLED

from (and by) Mick Inkpen

'Look!' your letter said,
'We want a poem for our book.'
'Representative of the best there is.'
'Not more than eight lines.'
'Preferably original.'
I, not a poet, blanked at the idea of verse.
Got in a state close to hysteria.
That's why it's late, and what's worse,
meets only one of your criteria.

UNTITLED

from (and by) Neil Innes

Like ice in a drink
Invisible ink
Or dreams in the cold light of day,
The children of Rock 'n' Roll
Never grow old
They just fade away ...

SOMEBODY ELSE

from (and by) Jackie Kay

If I was not myself, I would be somebody else.
But actually I am somebody else.
I have been somebody else all my life.
It is no laughing matter going about the place
all the time being somebody else:
people mistake you; you mistake yourself.

NAPOLEON

from (and by) Dillie Keane

Napoleon
Was lowly, an'
Littler
Than Hitler.

THE ELEPHANT

by A. E. Housman
(Henry Kelly's choice)

A tail behind, a trunk in front,
Complete the unusual elephant.
The tail in front, the trunk behind,
Is what you very seldom find.

THE DACHSHUND

(Sarah Kennedy's choice)

There was a Dachshund, once so long,
He hadn't any notion
How long it took to notify
His tail of his emotion;
And so it happened, while his eyes
Were filled with woe and sadness,
His little tail went wagging on
Because of previous gladness.

THE WAPITI

from (and by) Dick King-Smith

The American elk - also known as the wapiti -
Runs through the maple woods, clippety-cloppety.
Favoured with feet of remarkable property,
Wapitis never have need of chiropody.

Behold the happy moron
- He doesn't give a damn.
I wish I were a moron.
My God - perhaps I am!

And this one was taught me by my father:

I wish I were a cassowary
On the plains of Timbuctoo,
Then I'd eat a missionary,
Boots, and hat, and hymn book too.

P.S. Thought for the day:

*While on holiday I asked my wife if she knew that
"orange" is said to be the only word in English for
which there is no rhyme. She said: "You mean, like
'mortgage'?". And I think
she's right. I can't think of a rhyme for
mortgage either.*

**P.P.S. From the editors: And is there a rhyme
for "silver"?*

I'LL BE DARNED

(Gary Lineker's choice)

Said the toe to the sock,
'Let me through, let me through!'
Said the sock to the toe,
'I'll be darned if I do.'

CLOUDS

from (and by) Christopher Logue

First there is a mountain
Then there is no mountain
Then there is.

J.L: *Can I only have one choice?*

G.B: *Well ...*

J.L: *I think it could be one of these:*

AN ACCIDENT

'There's been an accident!' they said,
'Your husband's cut in half; he's dead!'
'Indeed!' said Mrs Brown, 'Well, if you please
Send me the half that's got my keys.'

UNTITLED

'I quite realized,' said Columbus,
'That the earth was not a
rhombus,
But I am a little annoyed
To find it an oblate spheroid.

MANIC-DEPRESSION

SOMETIMES I'M HAPPY
sometimes i'm sad
SoMeTiMeS i'M HsAaPdPY.

MONEY TALKS

by Richard Armour

That money talks,
I'll not deny,
I heard it once,
It said, 'Good-bye'.

ROBERT DeNIRO

by Louis Phillips

Robert DeNiro
Is a screen hero.
Only a slob
Would call him Bob.

VAN GOGH, VAN GOGH, VAN GOGH

It seems rather rough
On Vincent Van Guff
When those in the know
Call him Vincent Van Go
For unless I'm way off
He was Vincent Van Gogh.

THE BRITISH JOURNALIST

by Humbert Wolfe

You cannot hope to bribe or twist
Thank God! The British Journalist.
But seeing what the man will do
Unbribed, there's no occasion to.

THE ANSWER

by Leverett Lyon

I know just how to cure the world
And make it safe and stable;
But I haven't the time to do it,
And those that have, aren't able.

GOD AND THE DOCTOR

by John Owen

God and the Doctor we alike adore,
But only when in danger, not before;
The danger o'er, both are alike requited,
God is forgotten, and the doctor slighted.

UNTITLED

by G.F. Bowen

The rain it raineth on the just,
And also on the unjust fella;
But chiefly on the just, because,
The unjust steals the just's umbrella.

UNTITLED

People who live in Chateaux
Should never throw tomateaux

UNTITLED

by Artemus Ward

'Thrice is he armed
That hath his quarrel just.'
And four times he
Who gets his fist in fust.

THE PARENT

by Ogden Nash

Children aren't happy with nothing to
                                    ignore,
And that's what parents were created for.

A LITTLE GIRL I HATE

by Arnold Spilka

I saw a little girl I hate
And kicked her with my toes.
She turned
And smiled
And KISSED me!
Then she punched me in the nose.

HARD, HARD, HARD

It's hard to lose a friend
When your heart is full of hope;
But it's worse to lose a towel
When your eyes are full of soap.

EXCUSE

by Bruce Garrard

I stayed up late last night
eating
breakfast
in order to save time in the morning
but when I woke up I was hungry again
and so
I was late
for school.

NOAH'S ARK

When Noah sailed the waters blue,
He had his troubles, same as you.
For forty days he drove his ark
Before he found a place to park.

WE HEARD A POET TODAY

We heard a poet today.
He read some of his poems.
They weren't bad.
They were OK.
They were quite good really.
They were marvellous!

(I wish he'd stop looking over my
shoulder.)

J.L: ... but perhaps not.

DONT TELL PAPA

Magnus Magnusson's choice

Don't tell Papa his nose is red
As any rosebud or geranium;
Forbear to eye his hairless head
Or criticise his cootlike cranium;
'Tis years of sorrow and of care
Have made his head come through his hair.

UNTITLED

by Anon
(Michelle Magorian's choice)

I know a friendly brown eyed cow
That gives me milk and cheese
I'm lying in the nursery now
With foot and mouth disease

SITTING ON THE FENCE

by Michael Leunig
(Beverley Matthias's choice)

'Come sit down beside me,'
I said to myself,
And although it doesn't make sense,
I held my own hand
As a small sign of trust
And together I sat on the fence.

A NURSERY RHYME

(Sharon Maughan's choice)

Little Jack Horner
Sat in a corner,
Eating a bowl of rice.
He sat looking glum,
And then stuck out his tongue,
And did something that's not very nice.

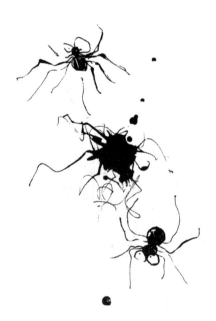

HISTORY

by Steve Turner
(Simon Mayo's choice)

History repeats itself.
Has to.
No one listens.

M m m m m m m m

from (and by) Mike McCartney

'M m m m m m m m' thought the blood red
poppy, as it stood in
the middle of the cornfield, waiting patiently
to be picked.

THE MONTHS

by George Ellis
(Trevor McDonald's choice)

Snowy, Flowy, Blowy,

Showery, Flowery, Bowery,

Hoppy, Croppy, Droppy,

Breezy, Sneezy, Freezy.

UNTITLED

from (and by) Roger McGough

to amuse
      emus
on warm summer nights

    Kiwis
do wiwis
from spectacular heights

IN GOOD HANDS

from (and by) Roger McGough

Wherever night falls
The earth is always there
To catch it.

GREAT HISTORICAL MISTAKES NO. 38

from (and by) Ian McMillan

Oh why
did I
invent
the wheel
right
at the top
of this
flipping
hill?

ODE TO THE INVISIBLE MAN

from (and by) Colin McNaughton

UNTITLED

(Paul Merton's choice)

Inspiration and genius aren't everything.
While Shakespeare wrote the phone didn't ring

BEATTIE IS THREE

from (and by) Adrian Mitchell

At the top of the stairs
I ask for her hand.
She gives it to me.
How her fist fits my palm
A bunch of consolation.
We take our time
Down the steep carpetway
As I wish, silently,
That the stairs were endless.

THE TOY SQUIRREL'S LAMENT

from (and by) John Mole

It's bad enough
To be stuffed
But it feels
Even worse on wheels.

SUSANNAH PROUT

by Walter de la Mare
(Bel Mooney's choice)

Here lies my wife,
Susannah Prout;
She was a shrew
I don't misdoubt;
But all I have
I'd give, could she
But for one hour
Come back to me.

LINES

by Mervyn Peake
(Elaine Moss's choice)

The sunlight falls upon the grass;
It falls upon the tower;
Upon my spectacles of brass
It falls with all its power.

It falls on everything it can,
For that is how it's made;
And it would fall on me, except,
That I am in the shade.

THE SUN

from (and by) Rory Motion

I stayed up all night
Thinking about the sun
Then in the morning
It dawned on me.

AN ATTEMPT AT THE SHORTEST POEM IN THE WORLD

from (and by) Gareth Owen

Already

This is too long!

CITY

by John Betjeman
(Michael Palin's choice)

When the great bell
BOOMS over the Portland stone urn, and
From the carved cedar wood
Rises the odour of incense,
I SIT DOWN
In St. Botolph Bishopsgate Churchyard
And wait for the spirit of my grandfather
Toddling along from the Barbican.

RABBIT'S SPRING

From (and by) Brian Patten

Snow
goes,

ice
thaws,

warm
paws!

LINES

by Tao Te Ching
(Jan Pienkowski's choice)

In dwelling, live close to the ground.
In thinking, keep to the simple.
In conflict, be fair and generous.
In governing, don't try to control.
In work, do what you enjoy.
In family life, be completely present.

SQUARE MEAL

by Adrian Henri
(Chris Powling's choice)

He kept a pet hyena
And then he bought a flock
He fed them all on Oxo cubes
And made a laughing stock.

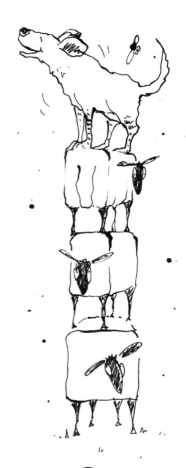

GOOD TASTE

by Adrian Mitchell
(Another Chris Powling choice)

The vilest furniture in this land
Is an elephant's foot umbrella stand.

GODLY

from (and by) Bernard Proctor

If God is not,
This much I wot:
He'll not remain a vacant lot
Aspiring to His Throne Divine
Are several acquaintances of mine.

THE LANE

from (and by) Simon Rae

Two cars graze together up a grassy lane.
A couple of farmers inspecting crops or stock?
Possibly, except it's already dusk and
                               threatening rain
And one of the cars begins, gently, to rock.

YOUTH

from (and by) Mike Read

You ask me 'Where did your youth go?'
'Why now so fast, when once so slow?'
The fairground burned, the piper played
It was you that went and youth that stayed.

I WISH

by Walter Raleigh
(Griff Rhys Jones's choice)

I wish I loved the human race,
I wish I loved its silly face,
I wish I loved the way it walks,
I wish I loved the way it talks,
And when I'm introduced to one
I wish I thought "what jolly fun!"

NEVER MIND

(Sir Tim Rice's choice)

Now all you young people come listen to me
When you take your vacation down by the
salt sea
If you wish for the fates and the Gods to be kind -
Ah never mind, never mind, never mind.

FOUR LIAM FOR LIAM

from (and by) Willy Russell

A boy who's bigger than tenpence
As marvellous as Christmas Eve
Taller than twelve jars of Marmite
As quick as a minibreve
As bright as a bottle of bluebells
As strong as four pairs of socks
A boy who's braver than Friday
And jacker than a Jack-In-The-Box
As lively as sasparilla
As clever as beans on toast
As bold as blue bananas
As quiet as Marley's ghost
A boy as sharp as lightening spears
And modest as the sea
Never ever was a boy before
A boy more four than me.

A POEM

by Spike Milligan
(Phillip Schofield's choice)

Said the mother Tern to her baby Tern
"Would you like a brother?"
Said the baby Tern to the mother Tern
"Yes. One good Tern deserves another."

THE ALLIGATOR WITH NO SHADOW

from (and by) Jo Shapcott

I used to have one
until a bad attack
of the hungers
came over me
and no living animal,
small or big,
was in jaw reach.
Snap. It tasted flat.

Lines from

IF

by Rudyard Kipling
(Dame Antoinette Sibley's choice)

If you can keep your head when all about you
   Are losing theirs and blaming it on you,
If you can trust yourself when all men doubt you,
   But make allowance for their doubting too;
If you can wait and not be tired by waiting,
   Or being lied about, don't deal in lies,
Or being hated, don't give way to hating,
   And yet don't look too good, nor talk too wise:

COMMUNION

from (and by) Frank Skinner

Walking towards the altar-rail
I looked back
At the still-seated, separate souls
Who'd killed a man
Or fallen out of love
Or had a crisp in the car.

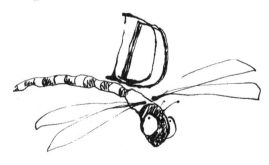

MISTER FROG

from (and by) Arthur Smith
(written age 8)

Mister Frog
Jumped out of the pond
Into the pouring rain
He said 'My word, it's cold and wet'
And jumped back in again.

Lines from

THE BEAST BITES BACK

from (and by) Ralph Steadman

Prowling in my sleep
Growling in the thunder of some godless dread
Filling in my tracks
The beast is on my back
Out of its tree
It follows me inside my head
It scratches on the skylight of my mind.

CONTENTMENT

by E. Clerihew Bentley
(Alec Stewart's choice)

I'm glad the sky is painted blue:
And the earth is painted green;
And such a lot of nice fresh air
All sandwiched in between.

THE FISHERMAN'S PRAYER

(Chris Tarrant's choice)

Lord give me grace
To catch a fish
So big, that
Even I ...
When talking of it
Afterwards,
Will never need
To lie ...

UNTITLED

from (and by) Sandi Toksvig

I always thought perhaps I could
Write a poem that was good
I meant to try yet was too slow
Till finally I had a go
Alas my thoughts moved like a hearse
As I feared it's gone from bad to verse.

BABY'S LAMENT

from (and by) Colin West

When Mum puts on
My nappy tight,
I somehow lose
My appetite.

COUSIN JANE

Also from (and by) Colin West

Yesterday my cousin Jane
Said she was an aeroplane,
But I wanted further proof -
So I pushed her off the roof.

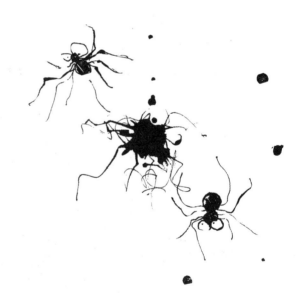

NURSERY RHYMES

(Paula Wilcox's choice)

Mary had a little lamb
Its fleece was black as soot,
And into Mary's bread and jam,
His sooty foot he put.

•

Hickory, dickory dock,
The mice ran up the clock,
The clock struck one;
The others escaped with minor injuries.

JUNGLE JINGLE

from (and by) Jacqueline Wilson

Lions leap, caterpillars creep,
And a panda will meander;
Rodents rustle, bison bustle,
But sloths are loth to move a muscle.

Lines from

ELEGY ON A COUNTRY CHURCHYARD

by Thomas Gray
(Terry Wogan's choice)

Full many a gem of purest ray serene
The dark unfathom'd caves of ocean bear:
Full many a flower is born to blush unseen,
And waste its sweetness on the desert air.

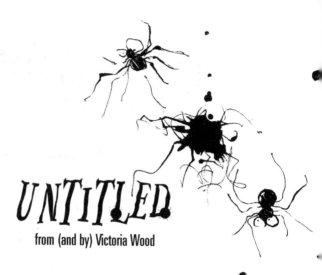

UNTITLED

from (and by) Victoria Wood

No rhyme!
No time!

A PAIR IN A HAMMOCK

A pair in a hammock
Attempted to kiss,
And in less than a jiffy
They landed like this.

APPLICATION

from (and by) Kit Wright

I'll pick for you two fuschia bells
From a bush in the greenwood clearing:
With the sap of a stem I'll fixify them
For an ear deserves an ear-ring!

Who's Who

From (and by) Benjamin Zephania

I used to think nurses
Were women,
I used to think police
Were men,
I used to think poets
Were boring,
Until I became one of them.

AFTERWORD
by Gyles Brandreth

I am no poet. I know it. I can prove it. Look:

ANIMAL CHATTER
A piece of doggerel by Gyles Brandreth

The other morning, feeling dog-tired, I was
walking sluggishly to school,
When I happened upon two girls I know - who
were busy playing the fool.
They were monkeying about, having a fight -
But all that they said didn't sound quite right.
'You're batty, you are - and you're catty too.'
'That's better than being ratty, you peevish shrew!'
'Don't be so waspish!' 'Don't be such a pig!'
'You silly goose! Let me have my say!'
'Why should I, you elephantine popinjay?!'
I stopped, I looked, I listened - and I had to laugh
Because I realised then, of course, it's never the
cow or the calf
That behave in this bovine way.
It's mulish humans like those girls I met the
other day.

(cont...)

121

You may think I'm too dogged, but something
                              fishy's going on -
The way we beastly people speak of animals is
                              definitely wrong.
Crabs are rarely crabby and mice are never mousey
(And I believe all lice deny that they are lousy).
You know, if I wasn't so sheepish and if I had

                                        my way
I'd report the English language to the RSPCA.

I may not be a proper poet like my friend Roger McGough
but, as you can see, I do like animals and I do like little
poems. Of all the little animal poems I've come across, these
are my favourites:

THE WISH

I wish I was a little grub
With whiskers round my tummy,
I'd climb into a honey-pot
And make my tummy gummy.

MAGGIE

There was a young lady named Maggie,
Whose dog was enormous and shaggy;
The front end of him
Looked vicious and grim -
But the back end was friendly and waggy.

THE HORSE

I know two things about the Horse,
And one of them is rather coarse.

MENAGERIE

The porcupine may have his quills,
  The elephant his trunk;
But when it comes to common scents,
  My money's on the skunk.

THE HIPPOPOTAMUS

Consider the poor hippopotamus:
His life is unduly monotonous.
He lives half asleep
At the edge of the deep,
And his face is as big as his bottom is.

RABBIT RACED A TURTLE

A rabbit raced a turtle,
You know the turtle won;
And Mister Bunny came in late,
A little hot cross bun!

A LITTLE WORM

by Spike Milligan

Today I saw a little worm
Wriggling on his belly.
Perhaps he'd like to come inside
And see what's on the Telly.

A CENTIPEDE

A centipede was happy quite,
Until a frog in fun
Said, 'Pray, which leg comes after which?'
This raised her mind to such a pitch,
She lay distracted in the ditch
Considering how to run.

At home we have always had animals. For a while, we had a very sophisticated French poodle called Phydeaux, and a lovely mongrel who thought his name was Down Boy. We had a cat called Oscar, who was wild, and another one called Thornton, who was worse. It was thanks to Oscar that, a few years ago, I wrote what was then the shortest poem in the history of the world. Ladislav Novák (see page 10) Gavin Ewart (see page 32) and Colin McNaughton (see page 85) have both beaten my record, but I think my poem is probably still the shortest *rhyming* piece of poetry. I came to write it when Oscar the cat ate Spot the goldfish. We were all very sad because we liked Spot and we had a little family memorial meeting at which we remembered him and I recited my poem. I hope you will like it, too.

ODE TO A GOLDFISH

by Gyles Brandreth

Oh
Wet
Pet!

That's it.

REACH

National Advice Centre
for Children with Reading Difficulties

Not being able to read is a hidden difficulty which affects many children and adults within every community. REACH was established in 1984, in memory of the children's writer, Enid Blyton, to assist children who have a difficulty with reading, writing, language and communication, and who may or may not have an additional sensory loss, motor or physical difficulty, intellectual or learning problem, behavioural or emotional disturbance. REACH offers expert and sympathetic practical help to families, teachers, librarians, carers and others responsible for the care and welfare of children. REACH believes that every child can and should be encouraged and stimulated to learn to read in whatever form and at whatever level is most appropriate for their needs. REACH has a well-stocked Resource Centre, a growing publications programme, presents in-service training courses to educationalists and other professionals within the area of child-care and works in a small number of schools in the Hampshire and Berkshire areas. REACH is totally dependent upon voluntary funding for its existence.

REACH: National Advice Centre for Children with
Reading Difficulties
California Country Park, Nine Mile Ride, Finchampstead,
Berkshire RG40 4HT
Tel: 0118 973 7575 (voice and text)
Fax: 0118 973 7105
E-mail: reach@reach-reading.demon.co.uk
Information Helpline: 0845 6040414

Acknowledgements

The editors and publishers extend their warm thanks to the contributors who have created poems or given permission to reproduce their poems in aid of the National Advice Centre for Children with Reading Difficulties, to whom all royalties are being donated. The copyright of all original contributions remains with the contributors.

Additionally, the editors and publishers gratefully acknowledge permission to reproduce the following copyright material: 'Young Poets' by Nicanor Parra, translated from the Spanish by Miller Williams, from *Poems One Line and Longer*, edited by William Cole, Grossman & Co, New York; 'Gloria' by Ladislav Novak and 'Silencio' by Eugen Gomringer from *An Anthology of Concrete Poetry*, edited by Emmett William, Something Else Press, New York; 'Silence' by Les Coleman from *Unthinking*, Littlewood Arc; 'Sausages' and 'The Fastest Train in the World' by Keith Bosley, from *Comic Verse*, edited by Roger McGough, Kingfisher Books; 'Famous Last' by Billy Bee, from Look, Times Newspapers Ltd; 'The Cow' and 'The Parent' by Ogden Nash, from *Selected Poems of Ogden Nash*, André Deutsch Ltd; 'Walking Away' by Cecil Day-Lewis, Jonathan Cape Ltd; 'Sitting on the Fence' by Michael Leuning, The Nation Review; 'Susannah Prout' by Walter de la Mare, The Society of Authors; 'Lines' by Mervyn Peake from *A Book of Nonsense*, Pan Books; 'City' by John Betjeman, John Murray Ltd; 'Said the Mother Tern', 'Pennies From Heaven' and 'A Little Worm' by Spike Milligan, Spike Milligan Productions.

While care has been taken to trace the owners of copyright material, in a few cases this has proved problematic and the editors and publishers take this opportunity to offer apologies to any copyright holders in any way not properly acknowledged and undertake to make appropriate corrections. Where no author is given for a poem, it is because the editors and publishers believe the authorship in question is unknown. However, if any poem published anonymously here has a known author who has not been acknowledged, the publishers undertake to make the appropriate correction.